Sharks

BY KARA L. LAUGHLIN

The Child's World®
childsworld.com

Published by The Child's World®
1980 Lookout Drive • Mankato, MN 56003-1705
800-599-READ • www.childsworld.com

DESIGN ELEMENTS
© creatOR76/Shutterstock.com: porthole
© keren-seg/Shutterstock.com: water

PHOTO CREDITS
© Andrea Izzotti/Shutterstock.com: 18-19; bikeriderlondon/Shutterstock.com: 20-21; Fiona Ayerst/Shutterstock.com: 14-15; Ingo Arndt/Minden Pictures: 12-13; Joe Quinn/Shutterstock.com: 11; Ramon Carretero/Shutterstock.com: 5; VisionDive/Shutterstock.com: 8-9, 17; wildestanimal/Shutterstock.com: cover, 1; Willyam Bradberry/Shutterstock.com: 6-7

ISBN: 9781503816923
LCCN: 2016945661

Printed in the United States of America
PA02326

NOTE FOR PARENTS AND TEACHERS

The Child's World® helps early readers develop their informational-reading skills by providing easy-to-read books that fascinate them and hold their interest. Encourage new readers by following these simple ideas:

BEFORE READING

- Page briefly through the book. Discuss the photos. What does the reader think he or she will learn in this book? Let the child ask questions.
- Look at the glossary together. Discuss the words.

READ THE BOOK

- Now read the book together, or let the child read the book independently.

AFTER READING

- Urge the child to think more. Ask questions such as, "What things are different among the animals shown in this book?"

Contents

Shark!

A big fish glides through the water. It has a mouth full of sharp teeth. The fish's **dorsal fin** breaks the surface. Then the fish dives down again. It is a shark!

Did you know?

There are more than 500 species of sharks.

Scales and Gills

Sharks live in every ocean of the world. They have two eyes and a long tail. They have fins to help them steer. Sharks have **scales**. They breathe with **gills**.

Did you know?
Sharks must keep water moving over their gills to breathe.

Speedy Sharks

Sharks are speedy. Their bodies have smooth curves. This lets them go fast.

Did you know?

Sharks can swim up to 24 miles (39 kilometers) per hour.

Sharks have **cartilage** instead of bones. Cartilage is strong and light. This keeps sharks quick.

Teeth

Sharks have rows and rows of teeth. Their teeth fall out easily. When one falls out, another grows into its place.

Did you know?

Sharks can have up to 30 rows of teeth!

Baby Sharks

Baby sharks are called **pups**. Some kinds of pups hatch from eggs. Others are born.

Shark mothers do not care for their pups. The pups must learn to eat and stay safe all by themselves.

Did you know?

Shark eggs are sometimes called "mermaids' purses."

On the Hunt

Sharks are fierce **predators**. They eat fish, seals, and even other sharks. Sharks use their **snouts** to feel and smell.

Did you know?

Sharks can smell prey up to 3 miles (5 kilometers) away.

Sharks can smell **prey** from miles away. They can also tell what is around them by feeling the water.

Sharks can feel **electric fields**. Hurt animals have strong electric fields. Sharks follow the fields to find the animals.

Did you know?

The small holes all over a shark's snout sense electric fields.

Dangers

Sharks are in trouble. Some people hunt them for food or medicine.

Some species were hunted too much. Now we have laws to protect sharks.

Sharks can look scary. But sharks are important animals. They keep the sea healthy.

Did you know?

Sharks live for about 30 years.

GLOSSARY

cartilage (KAR-tuh-lij): Cartilage is a bendable material that makes up certain body parts in animals and people.

dorsal fin (DOR-sull FIN): A fin on a sea animal's back is its dorsal fin.

electric fields (ee-LEK-trik FEELDZ): Electric fields are areas where electric energy is present. Your muscles make small electric fields when they work.

gills (GILLZ): Gills are openings on underwater animals that let the animals breathe underwater.

predators (PRED-uh-turz): Predators are animals that hunt other animals for food.

prey (PRAY): An animal that is hunted by other animals for food is prey.

pups (PUPS): Baby sharks are called pups.

scales (SKAYLZ): Scales are small, hard plates that cover some animals' skin.

snouts (SNOWTS): A snout is the nose area of an animal.

species (SPEE-sheez): A type of a certain animal. There are more than 500 species of sharks.

TO LEARN MORE

On the Web

Visit our Web page for lots of links about sharks:
www.childsworld.com/links

Note to parents, teachers, and librarians: We routinely verify our Web links to make sure they are safe, active sites—so encourage your readers to check them out!

In the Library

Brown, Skila. *Slickety Quick: Poems About Sharks.* Somerville, MA: Candlewick Press, 2016.

Harvey, Derek. *Super Shark Encyclopedia and Other Creatures of the Deep.* New York, NY: DK Publishing, 2015.

Musgrave, Ruth. *Everything Sharks (National Geographic Kids).* Washington, DC: National Geographic, 2011.

INDEX

About the Author

Kara L. Laughlin is an artist and writer who lives in Virginia with her husband, three kids, two guinea pigs, and a dog. She is the author of two dozen nonfiction books for kids.